FACTS ABOUT THE NEWT

By Lisa Strattin

© 2020 Lisa Strattin

FREE BOOK

FREE FOR ALL SUBSCRIBERS

LisaStrattin.com/Subscribe-Here

BOX SET

- FACTS ABOUT THE POISON DART FROGS
- FACTS ABOUT THE THREE TOED SLOTH
- FACTS ABOUT THE RED PANDA
- FACTS ABOUT THE SEAHORSE
- FACTS ABOUT THE PLATYPUS
- FACTS ABOUT THE REINDEER
- FACTS ABOUT THE PANTHER
- FACTS ABOUT THE SIBERIAN HUSKY

LisaStrattin.com/BookBundle

Facts for Kids Picture Books by Lisa Strattin

Little Blue Penguin, Vol 92

Chipmunk, Vol 5

Frilled Lizard, Vol 39

Blue and Gold Macaw, Vol 13

Poison Dart Frogs, Vol 50

Blue Tarantula, Vol 115

African Elephants, Vol 8

Amur Leopard, Vol 89

Sabre Tooth Tiger, Vol 167

Baboon, Vol 174

Sign Up for New Release Emails Here

http://LisaStrattin.com/subscribe-here

COVER IMAGE

Contents

INTRODUCTION

A Newt is a Salamander. They are semiaquatic. This means that they live in water and terrestrial habitats, depending on their stage of life. There are more than 100 known newt species around the world.

DISTRIBUTION

More than 100 known species of newts are found in
North America, Europe, North Africa and Asia.

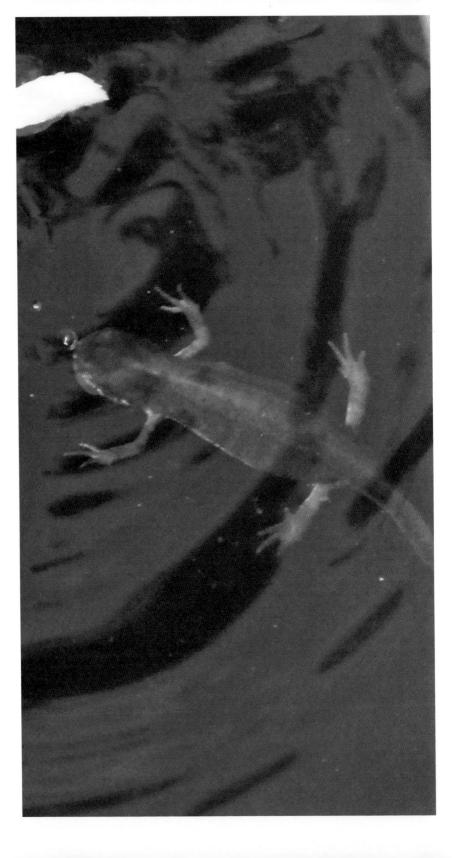

CHARACTERISTICS

Larvae Newts have gills to breathe underwater, four legs of equal size, a tail and glandular skin. There skin is not very smooth. They are able to grow a new leg if one is lost in a fight with another lizard or in an accident!

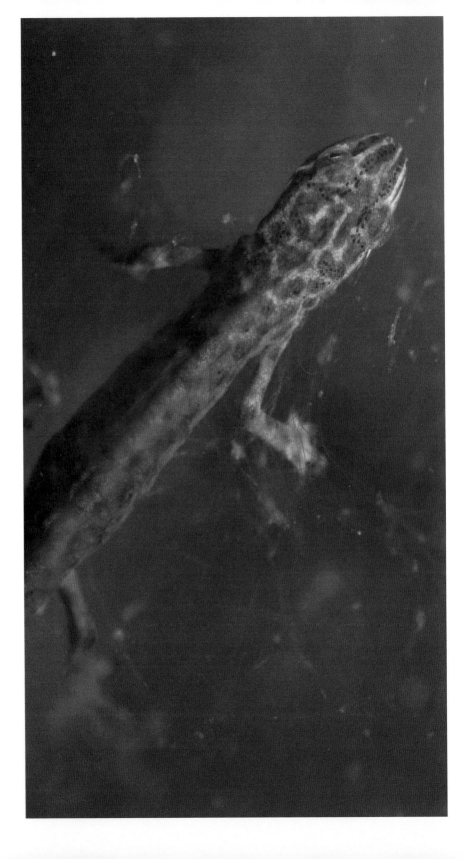

BREEDING / LIFE STAGES

Newts mainly breed during the months of June and July. The female lays single eggs, usually attaching the egg to an aquatic plant.

The larvae hatch in about three weeks. The Newt has three different life stages. They begin as aquatic larva, become terrestrial juvenile next, then grow to be adults.

Newts metamorphose through three distinct developmental life stages: aquatic larva, terrestrial juvenile (eft), and adult. As adults, they return to life in the water. This is what makes them semiaquatic salamanders.

LIFE SPAN

Depending on the species of Newt, they are known to live from 2 to 15 years.

SIZE

Some Newts are only 3 inches long, while others, like the Giant Crested Newt can grow to be 7 inches long!

HABITAT

Newts make their home in water and humid-land habitats (terrestrial) depending on the particular stage of life.

DIET

Newts are carnivores. On land, they are known to eat amphibian eggs, insects, worms and slugs. In the water, they eat shrimp, tadpoles and water insects. The babies, larvae, will eat insect larvae and small shrimp that they find swimming with them.

ENEMIES

Some Newts are able to secrete toxins that provide defense against predators. Some are even poisonous to humans, but only if the toxin is actually swallowed by people or comes into contact with a person's open sore.

SUITABILITY AS PETS

There are a number of Newt species that are kept as pets. The best way to choose one is to visit a reptile shop that is able to give you some guidance on which one to select for yourself.

COLOR ME

COLOR ME

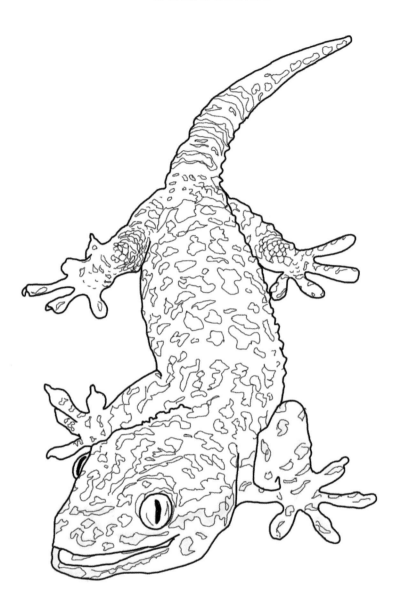

COLOR ME

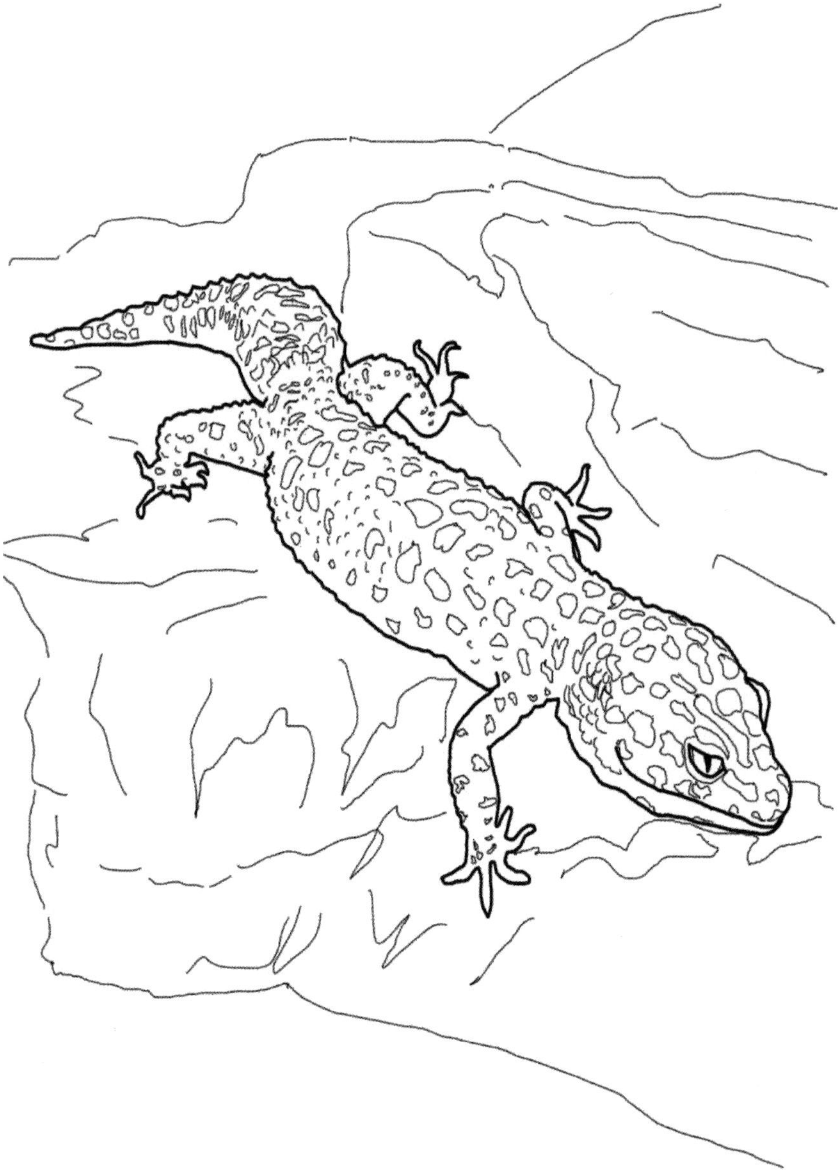

COLOR ME

COLOR ME

COLOR ME

COLOR ME

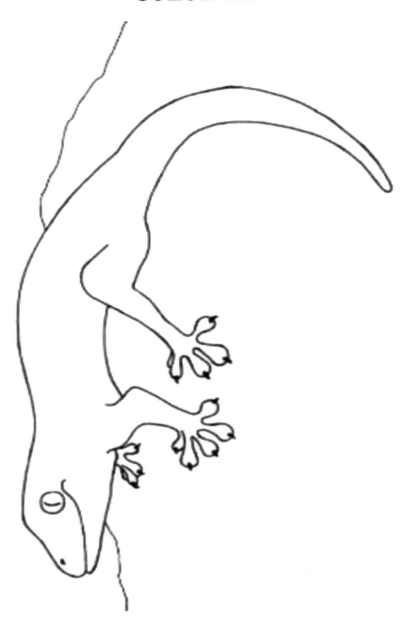

COLOR ME

COLOR ME

Please leave me a review here:

LisaStrattin.com/Review-Volume-381

For more Kindle Downloads Visit Lisa Strattin Author Page on Amazon Author Central

amazon.com/author/lisastrattin

To see upcoming titles, visit my website at LisaStrattin.com– all books available on kindle!

lisastrattin.com

FREE BOOK

Printed in Great Britain
by Amazon

41820132R00024